COUNTRY EXPLORERS

ITALY

Madeline Donaldson

Lerner Publications Company • Minneapolis

For my nephew Joseph and his Italian grandmother, Bianca

Lerner Publications Company
A division of Lerner Publishing Group, Inc.
241 First Avenue North
Minneapolis, MN 55401 U.S.A.

Website address: www.lernerbooks.com

Library of Congress Cataloging-in-Publication Data

Donaldson, Madeline.
    Italy / by Madeline Donaldson.
       p. cm. — (Country explorers)
    Includes index.
    ISBN 978–0–7613–5316–4 (lib. bdg. : alk. paper)
    1. Italy—Juvenile literature. I. Title.
DG417.D66 2011
945—dc22   2009042333

Manufactured in the United States of America
1 – VI – 7/15/10

Table of Contents

Welcome! 4

Hills and Mountains 6

Water Everywhere 8

Lots of Farmland 10

All Weather 12

The Romans 14

Italy Comes Back 16

Becoming One Italy 18

The Italians 20

City Life 22

Country Life 24

Getting Around 26

All in the Family 28

Let's Eat! 30

School Six Days a Week 32

Religion 34

Time Off 36

Kick It! 38

Folk Arts and Music 40

Invent This! 42

The Flag of Italy 44

Fast Facts 45

Glossary 46

To Learn More 47

Index 48

Welcome!

Italy sits on the continent of Europe. The country is long and narrow. It is shaped like a tall boot. The Mediterranean Sea surrounds three sides of the boot. Northern Italy touches France, Monaco, Switzerland, Austria, and Slovenia. Two large islands are also part of Italy. Sardinia lies west of Italy. Sicily nearly touches the toe of Italy's boot.

Two Small Countries

Two very small countries are tucked inside Italy. They rule themselves. Vatican City is in Rome, Italy's capital. San Marino is in central Italy.

Sicily is the largest island in the Mediterranean Sea. Mount Etna rises in the background.

SWITZERLAND

AUSTRIA

SLOVENIA

LAKE
MAGGIORE

LAKE
COMO

ALPS

ALPS

ALPS

ALPS

LAKE DISTRICT

LAKE
GARDA

Venice

Turin

Milan

PO RIVER

PO VALLEY

FRANCE

Genoa

APENNINES

Bologna

SAN
MARINO

MONACO

Florence

Pisa

ARNO RIVER

Siena

ITALY

N

ADRIATIC
SEA

MEDITERRANEAN
SEA

TIBER RIVER

APENNINES

VATICAN
CITY

★ Rome

Bari

TYRRHENIAN
SEA

Naples

Pompeii

MOUNT
VESUVIUS

SARDINIA

IONIAN
SEA

	mountains
	volcano
★	country's capital
•	city

MILES

0   100

0   100

KILOMETERS

SICILY

MOUNT
ETNA

Italy

A skier climbs the peak of a mountain in the Dolomites, a section of the Alps.

Hills and Mountains

Mountains cover much of Italy. The Alps curve around northern Italy. These mountains also reach into France, Switzerland, and Austria. Skiing in the Alps is a favorite winter sport.

The Apennines run down central Italy. They reach from north to south. Valleys and plains lie on both sides of the mountains. Hilly areas are also to the west. These areas form some of Italy's best farmland.

Map Whiz Quiz

Take a look at the map on page 5. A map is a drawing or chart of a place. Trace the outline of Italy on a sheet of paper. Can you find the Alps? Mark them with an *N* for north. Do you see Sardinia? Mark the island with a *W* for west. Put an *E* for east on the Adriatic Sea. With a green crayon, color in Italy. Don't forget Sardinia and Sicily! And be sure to black out San Marino and Vatican City. They don't belong to Italy.

This town lies in central Italy. Lush farmland surrounds it.

Water Everywhere

Italy is a peninsula. This means it has water on three sides. The country also has lots of rivers. Many of them flow down from the mountains. They bring water to farmland.

The Po River runs through the city of Turin. Buildings line the riverbanks.

The Po is Italy's longest river. It runs across northern Italy. Other rivers are the Arno and the Tiber. The Arno is the main river in central Italy. The Tiber flows into Rome in central Italy.

Lake District

Long ago, slow-moving ice masses carved out lakes in the Alps. The narrow lakes filled with melted snow. They formed the Lake District. Lake Como, Lake Garda, and Lake Maggiore draw many visitors every year.

Windsurfers enjoy the water at Lake Como. It is the third-largest lake in Italy.

Lots of Farmland

The Po River flows into the largest valley in Italy. Farmers have been planting and watering crops in the Po Valley for thousands of years. The main crops are wheat, corn, rice, grapes, sugar beets, and potatoes.

The Po Valley lies across northern Italy. The valley holds some of Italy's best farmland.

People also farm land on either side of the Apennines. Farmers tend grapes, wheat, tomatoes, peppers, and fruit and olive trees. Farms in the far south and Sicily grow citrus fruits, such as lemons and oranges.

It's harvesttime at this fruit orchard. These tangerines are ready for the market.

All Weather

Italy gets just about every kind of weather. Skiers love the snow that falls in the north. Farms throughout the country get rain in spring. Melting snow also swells rivers that water farmland.

Children awake to an overnight snowfall in Siena, Italy. They sled in a town square.

12

Both visitors and Italians enjoy the sunny days of summer. Beaches draw huge crowds. People can walk among old buildings or sit in large squares. Open-air restaurants get lots of business in summer.

Volcanoes

Italy has some of Europe's largest volcanoes. A few still spew hot ash and lava. Mount Etna on Sicily is still active. It erupts (blows up) at least once a year. Mount Vesuvius is near Naples. This volcano last erupted in 1944.

People enjoy good food and a beautiful view of Lake Garda, near the Alps.

Long ago, Romans ruled Italy. This image of ancient Romans is carved in marble.

The Romans

People have lived in Italy for a long, long time. One of the most famous groups of people was the Romans. They ruled a huge empire in Italy about two thousand years ago. Then they spread their way of life far and wide. Over time, the Romans ruled parts of Europe, Africa, and Asia.

14

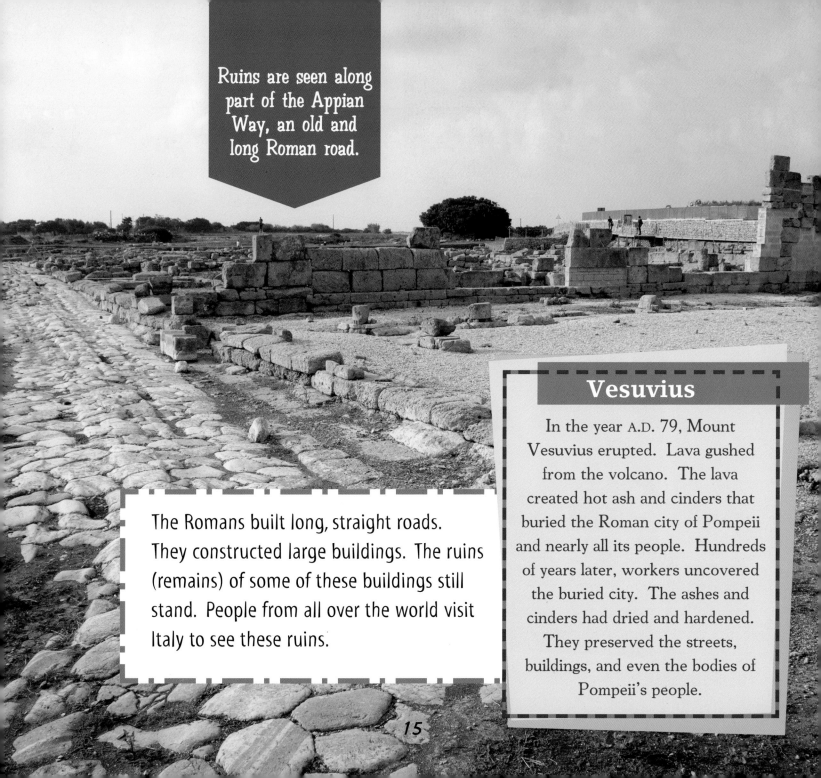

Ruins are seen along part of the Appian Way, an old and long Roman road.

Vesuvius

In the year A.D. 79, Mount Vesuvius erupted. Lava gushed from the volcano. The lava created hot ash and cinders that buried the Roman city of Pompeii and nearly all its people. Hundreds of years later, workers uncovered the buried city. The ashes and cinders had dried and hardened. They preserved the streets, buildings, and even the bodies of Pompeii's people.

The Romans built long, straight roads. They constructed large buildings. The ruins (remains) of some of these buildings still stand. People from all over the world visit Italy to see these ruins.

15

Italy Comes Back

About fifteen hundred years ago, the Roman Empire fell apart. Over time, dukes, princes, and kings ruled smaller areas of land.

Modern banking began in Italy. This painting from 1400 shows a countinghouse (bank) in Florence.

The painting shows the life of wealthy people in the city of Venice during the 1400s.

Famous Artists

Some Italian artists are famous around the world. Leonardo da Vinci painted, sculpted, and invented. Michelangelo did too. Their works are in museums in Italy and other countries.

Cities such as Florence, Milan, and Venice became important centers of business for these areas. Business leaders hired artists to make the cities look good. The artists painted, sculpted, and constructed buildings. By the 1400s, Italy was showing off its wealth.

Napoleon Bonaparte of France invades Italy in 1796.

Becoming One Italy

Italy remained just a group of separate areas for hundreds of years. The country was not united. By the 1800s, some Italians were working to bring the areas of Italy together.

By 1870, all the different areas of Italy joined together. They formed the kingdom of Italy. Italians later decided they didn't want a king. So a leader called the prime minister runs the country.

North and South

Many factories are in northern Italy. Workers there make cars, machinery, shoes, and fabrics. Farming is the main business in southern Italy. People in the north and the south often have different opinions. They don't always agree on how Italy should be run.

General Giuseppe Garibaldi (left) helped Italy unite.

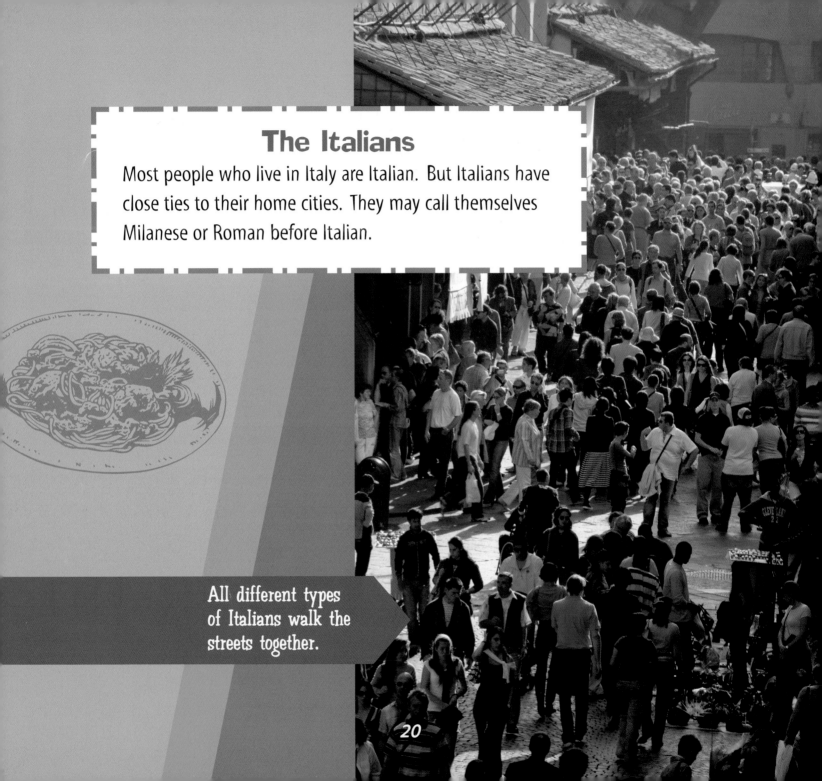

The Italians

Most people who live in Italy are Italian. But Italians have close ties to their home cities. They may call themselves Milanese or Roman before Italian.

All different types of Italians walk the streets together.

20

Italian is the national language. But accents (ways of speaking) change from one area to another. Young Italians learn English in school. Older Italians might also speak French.

Newcomers

New people have come to Italy. Most have come from nearby countries, such as Greece or Albania. They brought their languages, religions, and ways of life with them.

A man reads *Il Gazzettino*, an Italian newspaper.

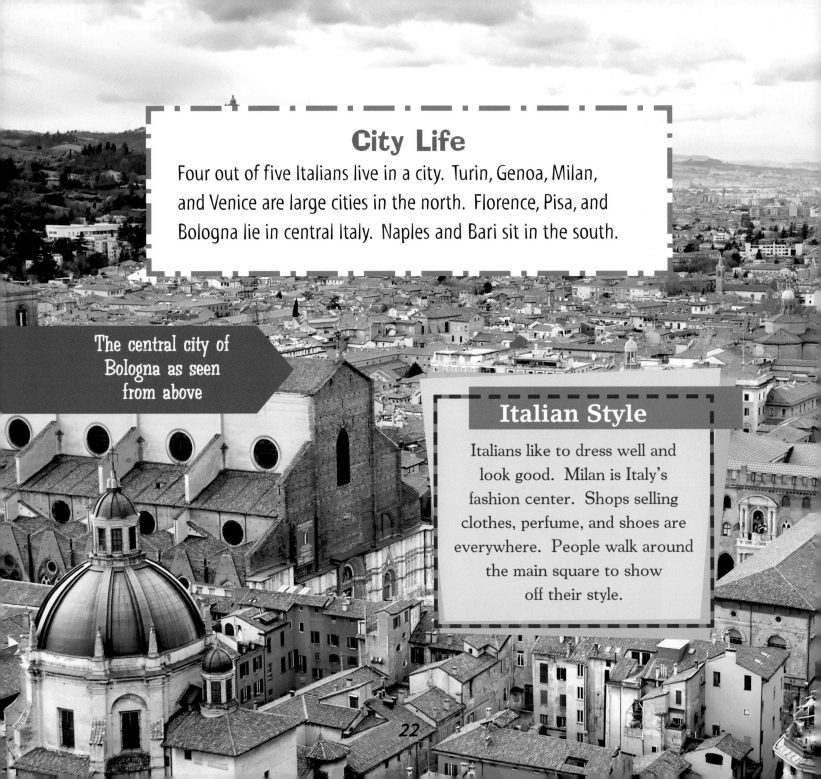

City Life

Four out of five Italians live in a city. Turin, Genoa, Milan, and Venice are large cities in the north. Florence, Pisa, and Bologna lie in central Italy. Naples and Bari sit in the south.

The central city of Bologna as seen from above

Italian Style

Italians like to dress well and look good. Milan is Italy's fashion center. Shops selling clothes, perfume, and shoes are everywhere. People walk around the main square to show off their style.

Rome, the capital, is the largest city. But each part of the country has a major center.

Dear Aunt Mary,
The old buildings in Rome are awesome. Yesterday we saw the Colosseum. That's one huge outdoor theater. The ancient Romans built it almost two thousand years ago! Imagine that. Afterward, we stopped for yummy gelato ice cream.
See you soon,
Clare

Y
Y
An

Rome, Italy

Country Life

Only one in five Italians lives in the countryside. Country life is slow. Shops close for several hours while people eat lunch at midday. People gather in small squares to visit.

A group of men sit together and chat.

The small town of Vernazza sits on a hill near the sea.

Many villages and small towns are hundreds of years old. They might hug cliffs that overlook the sea. Or they might sit in the middle of rich farmland.

People board a train
at a station
in Naples.

Uscita →

Getting Around

Many Italians use buses and trains to get around. They can ride subways in Rome, Milan, and Naples. In the country, people often walk to shops and to visit friends.

Venice

Venice is a major port in northeastern Italy. The city is built on small islands. Narrow waterways called canals snake between the islands. No cars are allowed on most of the islands in Venice. Instead, people walk or get around on boats.

Italy makes a lot of cars. So Italians also drive to get around. You'll see many scooters zipping between the cars too.

Scooters are a popular way to get around.

27

All in the Family

Italian families are close. Children feel the love of all the family members. Adults may live with their parents until they marry. Grandparents are respected and cared for.

Many generations of an Italian family get together. Family is important to Italians.

Family members help kids find jobs or pay for schooling. Older people may help care for the children of working parents. Grandparents, parents, aunts, uncles, and kids often get together for meals.

Mamma Mia!

Mothers are important in Italian families. They hold families together. They make sure family members help one another.

Many members of this family eat dinner together outside.

29

Let's Eat!

Italy is famous for its food. Pasta and rice are everywhere. At a main meal, pasta or rice is usually eaten first. Meat or fish and vegetables, such as salad, come next. Sometimes a meal might start with many different kinds of olives and sliced salami and ham. Meals often end with fresh fruit.

An Italian family eats pasta during dinner.

Pizza started in Naples. The crusts are thin. Very little sauce and few toppings are used. Some of Italy's great cheeses finish off the pizza. Then it is baked in an oven heated with wood. Italians eat pizza as a snack.

Screaming for Gelato

On a hot summer day, nothing cools like gelato. This Italian ice cream comes in many flavors, from chocolate to sour cherry.

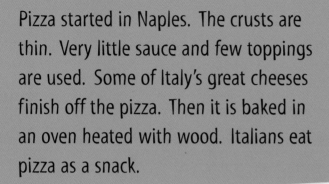

Cooks take out freshly baked pizzas from a wood oven in Naples.

School Six Days a Week

Italian kids start school at the age of six. They go to school six days a week. But they get out early in the afternoon. Most schools don't have after-school activities. Kids just go home. They do lots of homework.

A student does schoolwork at her desk.

At the age of fourteen, students take a test. The test tells them what kind of high school they should choose. Some schools lead to college. Other schools teach skills that lead to a job.

Look, Touch, and Learn

Maria Montessori was an Italian teacher. She had new ideas about teaching and learning. Montessori thought kids would learn better if they could work at their own pace. She also thought kids learn by using hands-on toys.

High school students listen to their teacher during a trip to an Italian museum.

33

Italians celebrate Easter at Santa Maria del Fiore Cathedral in Florence.

Religion

Most Italians belong to the Roman Catholic Church. Its center is in Vatican City. People go to their local church to celebrate births and marriages and to remember those who have died. Easter is the most important church holiday. People go to church on Easter Sunday. Then families relax on Easter Monday, the day after Easter.

Italians celebrate the Christmas season from December 24 through January 6. On the last day, a kind witch called la Befana brings gifts.

Girls wear Befana outfits during a parade for the holiday.

35

Time Off

Many Italians spend the whole month of August on vacation. They travel to the countryside or the beach. They relax with family and friends.

An Italian family eats outside during their August vacation.

Meanwhile, visitors flock to Italy's cities. They walk in public squares. They enjoy Italian food at outdoor restaurants. They visit museums and Roman ruins.

Tourists do some sightseeing in Florence, Italy.

Horse Racing Festivals

The city of Siena has a famous horse race in the summer. The neighborhoods of the city compete to win the racing prize. Another horse race takes place on Sardinia. It honors a military victory from Roman times.

An Italian soccer team celebrates their win along with their fans.

Kick It!

Soccer is the king of sports in Italy. Thousands of noisy fans crowd stadiums. They cheer for their favorite team. The Italian national team has won soccer's World Cup three times.

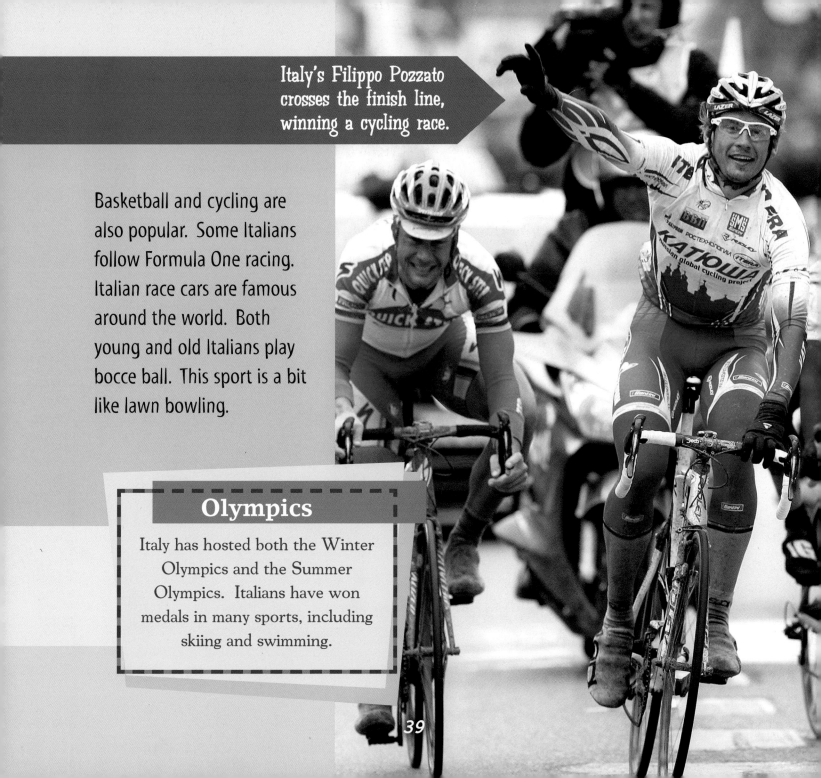

Basketball and cycling are also popular. Some Italians follow Formula One racing. Italian race cars are famous around the world. Both young and old Italians play bocce ball. This sport is a bit like lawn bowling.

Olympics

Italy has hosted both the Winter Olympics and the Summer Olympics. Italians have won medals in many sports, including skiing and swimming.

39

Folk Arts and Music

Italians are skilled at making useful crafts. Visit any marketplace in Italy. You'll see tiles, vases, and other colorful works. Goods made of leather, iron, and wood are also popular.

Pottery shops are favorite tourist spots.

Operas tell stories. They use acting, scenery, and costumes as plays do. But operas use music and singing to tell the story. Words are sung, not spoken. Italians wrote some of the world's best operas. And Italian opera singers are known around the world. La Scala in Milan is one of the world's most famous opera houses.

Opera performers entertain the audience on the stage at La Scala.

Invent This!

Italians are creative and clever. Leonardo da Vinci drew plans for flying machines, tanks, and weapons in the 1400s. Modern-day people have built his inventions. They work!

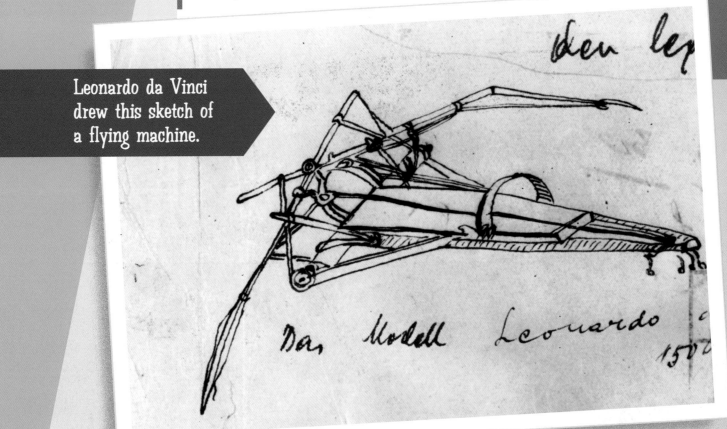

Leonardo da Vinci drew this sketch of a flying machine.

Italian astronomer Galileo Galilei looks into the sky with a telescope.

Marconi

In the late 1800s, Guglielmo Marconi invented a wireless way to send messages. His creation became the telegraph. His studies later helped radio and TV get started.

In the 1600s, Galileo Galilei was the first person to use a telescope to study the night sky. And Alessandro Volta invented the first battery in 1800.

THE FLAG OF ITALY

Italy's flag has three colored bands. They are green, white, and red. People have different ideas about what the colors mean. One view is that green stands for hope. White is for peace or purity. And red stands for bravery. Another thought is that green stands for the plains and hills of the Italian countryside. White is the Alps. And red is for the blood spilled to unite Italy.

FAST FACTS

FULL COUNTRY NAME: Italian Republic

AREA: 116,320 square miles (301,269 square kilometers), or a bit smaller than the state of New Mexico

MAIN LANDFORMS: the mountain ranges Alps and Apennines; the valley Po; the volcanoes Mount Etna and Mount Vesuvius

MAJOR RIVERS: Po, Arno, and Tiber

ANIMALS AND THEIR HABITATS: brown bears, chamois, foxes, ibex, roe deer (the Alps); great spotted woodpeckers, otters, peregrine falcons, wolves (Apennines); golden eagles, great black woodpeckers (southern Italy); mouflon sheep, wild boars (Sardinia)

CAPITAL CITY: Rome

OFFICIAL LANGUAGE: Italian

POPULATION: about 59,900,000

GLOSSARY

ancient: having been around for a long time; very old

canal: a narrow waterway

capital: a city where the government of a state or country is located

continent: any one of seven large areas of land. The continents are Africa, Antarctica, Asia, Australia, Europe, North America, and South America.

empire: a large area ruled by an emperor or empress

goods: things to sell

map: a drawing or chart of all or part of Earth or the sky

mountain: a part of Earth's surface that rises high into the sky

opera: a play in which the actors sing, not say, their lines

prime minister: a political leader who runs a country

sculpt: to shape blocks of stone or wood with tools

telegraph: a machine that sends messages without using wires

telescope: a tool used to view distant objects, such as stars in the sky

valley: an area of low ground that gets its water from a large river

volcano: a crack in Earth's surface through which hot gases, lava, and ash can blow

TO LEARN MORE

BOOKS

Adler, David A. *Fun with Roman Numerals*. New York: Holiday House, 2008. This book shows ways we still use ancient Roman numbers in daily life.

Sonneborn, Liz. *The Romans: Life in Ancient Rome*. Minneapolis: Millbrook Press, 2010. The fresh artwork in this book gives kids a modern window into the lives of the ancient Romans.

Walker, Sally M. *Volcanoes*. Minneapolis: Lerner Publications Company, 2008. Learn what makes volcanoes erupt in this fascinating book.

Wheeler, Lisa. *Dino-Soccer*. Minneapolis: Carolrhoda Books, 2009. Soccer fans everywhere will cheer from the sidelines for their favorite dino team.

WEBSITES

Ancient Rome for Kids
http://rome.mrdonn.org
This site shares all kinds of information about ancient Rome.

Enchanted Learning
http://www.enchantedlearning.com/geography
This site has pages to label and color of Italy and its flag.

Time for Kids
http://www.timeforkids.com/TFK/kids/hh/goplaces/main/0,28375,726880,00.html
This general site has a section on Italy that includes a quiz, pictures, and a timeline.

INDEX

arts, 17, 40–41

cities, 17, 22, 26–27

families, 28–29
farmers, 10–11
flag, 44
food, 30–31

inventions, 42–43

language, 21

map, 5

people, 20–21

religion, 34–35
rivers, 8–9
Romans, 14–15
Rome, 4–5, 23

schools, 32–33
sightseeing, 37
sports, 6, 38–39

The photographs in this book are used with the permission of: © Ales Liska/Shutterstock Images, p. 4; © Bill Hauser/Independent Picture Service, pp 5, 44; © Andreas Strauss/LOOK/Getty Images, p. 6; © epsylon_lyrae/Shutterstock Images, p. 7; © DEA Picture Library/Getty Images, p. 8; © Malcolm McLeod/Alamy, p. 9; © vesilvio/Shutterstock Images, p. 10; © Francesco Ruggeri/The image Bank/Getty Images, p. 11; © Franco Origlia/Getty Images, p. 12; © Harold Eisenberger/LOOK/Getty Images, p. 13; © iStockphoto.com/Angelafoto, p. 14; © David Epperson/Digital Vision/Getty Images, p. 15; The Granger Collection, New York, p. 16; © Cameraphoto Arte, Venice/Art Resource, NY, p. 17 (top); © Erich Lessing/Art Resource, NY, p. 17 (bottom); Rue des Archives / The Granger Collection, New York, p. 18; © Topical Press Agency/Getty Images, p. 19; © Annie Griffiths Belt/National Geographic/Getty Images, p. 20; © Supated/Alamy, p. 21; © iStockphoto.com/maria luisa berti, p. 22; © Tiziana Fabi/AFP/Getty Images, pp. 23, 35; © Y. Levy/Alamy, p. 24; © Julie Eggers/DanitaDelimont.com, p. 25; © Atlantide Phototravel/CORBIS, pp. 26,34; © Oliviero Olivieri/Robert Harding Travel/Photolibrary, p. 27; Henrick Sorensen/Riser/Getty Images, p. 28; © Adrian Weinbrecht/Digital Vision/Getty Images, p. 29; © Stephanie Maze/CORBIS, p. 30; © Jon Spauli/Photolibrary, p. 31 (left); © Philip and Karen Smith/Iconica/Getty Images, p. 31 (right); © Annie Griffiths Belt/CORBIS, p. 32; © Martin Thomas Photography/Alamy, p. 33; Reflexstock/Image Source, p. 36; © David Ball/CORBIS, p. 37; © Massimo Cebrelli/Getty Images, p. 38; © Yves Herman/Reuters/CORBIS, p. 39; ©Christine Webb/Alamy, p. 40; © Handout/Reuters/CORBIS, p. 41; © Hulton Archive/Getty Images, pp. 42, 43.

Front cover: © Guy Vanderelst/Photographers Choice/Getty Images.